Patmos Speaks Today

John Weston

Scripture Truth Publications

PATMOS SPEAKS TODAY

First published as articles in the magazine "Scripture Truth" 2000-02.

FIRST EDITION

FIRST PUBLISHED February 2007

ISBN: 978-0-901860-66-8

© Copyright 2007 John Weston/Scripture Truth

A publication of Scripture Truth

All rights reserved. No part of this publication may be reproduced, stored in a retrieval system, or transmitted, in any form or by any means, electronic, mechanical, photocopying, recording or otherwise without prior permission of Scripture Truth Publications.

Scripture quotations, unless otherwise indicated, are taken from The Authorized (King James) Version. Rights in the Authorized Version are vested in the Crown. Reproduced by permission of the Crown's patentee, Cambridge University Press.

Cover photograph ©iStockphoto.com/JMWScout (Mark Weiss)

Published by Scripture Truth Publications
Coopies Way, Coopies Lane,
Morpeth, Northumberland, NE61 6JN

Scripture Truth is an imprint of Central Bible Hammond Trust, a charitable trust

Typesetting by John Rice
Printed by Lightning Source

Contents

    Personal profile of the author 5
1. Introduction 7
2. The Letters to the Seven Churches 20
3. Ephesus 23
4. Smyrna 27
5. Pergamum 33
6. Thyatira 39
7. Sardis 45
8. Philadelphia 51
9. Laodicea 57
10. A Collective View of the Seven Churches 66

PATMOS SPEAKS TODAY

Personal Profile

JOHN ALLEN WESTON, born 1920, son of John and Daisy Weston.

John Weston Senior ministered at Wildfell Hall, Catford, South London for 50 years. The building had been given to him in 1912 by his future father-in-law to serve as a base for his evangelistic ministry.

John Allen lectured in Colleges of Horticulture, and for 15 years was Senior Warden of the Kent Horticultural Institute. It was during this period (1956) that John had a strong desire that Wildfell Hall should become a centre for Bible teaching. It was already an acknowledged centre for evangelistic outreach; it should now feed the Body of Christ in South London. To this end, John coined the title phrase 'The Catford Lectures' and commenced organising monthly Bible addresses. These were initially directed towards local churches who responded in large numbers.

In 1971, he was appointed National Management Training Advisor with the Agricultural Training Board. He was also Senior Examiner in Horticultural Management for the City and Guilds of London.

However in 1973, following the tragic death of their son in 1971, John and Margaret moved to Jerusalem to serve with the Churches Ministry to the Jewish People. While in Israel, John was privileged to participate in Agricultural Training programmes organised by the Israeli Ministry of Agriculture.

Later, John joined FEBA Radio, the British missionary radio organisation. He travelled extensively throughout the United Kingdom, Europe, as well as India, Pakistan and the Seychelles. Apart from various individual broadcasts, including television, John was invited by the

BBC to give two series of weekly meditations. He retired from FEBA in 1985 but continued an active Bible teaching ministry, in the United Kingdom, Europe and the U.S.A.

Israel, though, remained his first love. Apart from their 25 years involvement in Holy Land pilgrimages, Margaret and John have led tours in 'The Steps of Paul' and to 'The Seven Churches' including the Isle of Patmos. This book is based on talks given at the various biblical sites on the latter tours.

1. Introduction

JOHN ON PATMOS

Patmos, the Jerusalem of the Aegean, is a beautiful island nestling in blue waters. It forms one of the islands of the Dodecanese about 150 km. (90 miles) across the sea from the ruins of Ephesus in Turkey. Patmos covers about 35 sq.km. (13 sq. miles), with a distance of 15 km. (9 miles) from north to south. Visiting Patmos is one of the great delights of life. Here is a peaceful, holy, island with many picturesque bays. Standing in one of them, watching a glorious sunset, is an unforgettable experience.

However, it is the biblical aspect which has highlighted this island and the one which draws so many Christian visitors. Here, in around AD 95, the apostle John was taken as a prisoner and exiled for one and a half years. It was here, during his imprisonment, that he received what we now call 'The Revelation', the last book of the Bible, telling of those things which were to come to pass.

John's experience, while here on Patmos, reflects the age-old saying, "Two men looking through the bars, one saw mud, the other saw stars". Some 30 years before John's exile, Seneca was banished to Corsica. All he could write was, "A living death, nothing here but exile and an exile's grave." But not so with John! It was not for him to exclaim, "Why has this happened to me?", but rather, "How can I respond to this situation?" We sense no bitterness, no blind resignation but, instead, a spirit of ecstasy as he recounts the vision which unfolded before his eyes.

Visiting Patmos, standing or kneeling in the cave where all this took place, we recall how John Bunyan turned his cell into a sanctuary, and gave us 'Pilgrim's Progress'. We recall how the cell of Paul and Silas in Philippi likewise became a sanctuary, and echoed and re-echoed with hymns of praise (Acts 16:25). Samuel Rutherford, too, could write while in prison,

> *E'en Anworth was not heaven;*
> *E'en preaching was not Christ.*
> *But in my sea-beat prison*
> *My Lord and I held tryst.*
> *And aye my murkiest storm cloud*
> *Was by a rainbow spanned,*
> *Caught from the glory dwelling*
> *In Immanuel's land.*

So, in his cell on Patmos, John heard songs of worship and praise. These must surely have lifted up his spirit and brought a radiance to his prison cell. These songs are to be found in chapters 4 and 5 of Revelation. In 4:11, we have a song with three basic strands: "Thou art worthy, O Lord, to receive *glory* and *honour* and *power*". These three strands indicate praise to the triune God, seated upon the throne. At the close of chapter 5, there is a song with four strands. In Scripture, the number four generally reflects universality. This universality is seen in the fourfold origin of the singers: "every creature which is in heaven, and on the earth, and under the earth, and such as are in the sea, and all that are in them, heard I saying, Blessing, and honour, and glory, and power, be unto him that sitteth upon the throne, and unto the Lamb for ever and ever" (verse 13).

The singers add the word 'blessing' to the 'glory, honour and power' in their song directed to the Lamb. Why so? Of those long centuries which followed the fall of man, Scripture tells us, "the whole creation groaneth and travaileth in pain" (Romans 8:22). But now all this has changed! It is to the Lamb that this song of praise is rendered. Through His victory the curse has been lifted; through His victory the powers of evil have been defeated. The curse has been changed to blessing!

> *The whole creation joins in one*
> *To bless the sacred Name*
> *Of Him who sits upon the throne*
> *And to adore the Lamb.*

However, the topmost heights of worship are reached in the sevenfold song of the redeemed: "Worthy is the Lamb that was slain to receive *power*, and *riches*, and *wisdom*, and *strength*, and *honour*, and *glory*, and *blessing*" (verse 12). This song includes the basic strand of 'glory, honour and power', it celebrates the blessing to the whole of creation, but then introduces three further strands.

The threefold addition to this hymn of adoration and worship is so precious. It is peculiar to the redeemed. Let's think about each of these strands.

riches – reminding us of Him who was rich beyond all telling, yet became so poor for us, so that through His poverty we might be rich (2 Corinthians 8:9). Here, at last, is the glorious answer to Calvary's poverty!

wisdom – speaking of the One who, by His wisdom, delivered us from the wrath to come. We are reminded of the poor, wise man: "He by his wisdom delivered the city" (Ecclesiastes 9:14-15). We recall, too, that "the preaching of the cross is to them that perish foolishness; but unto us which are saved it is the power of God" (1 Corinthians 1:18).

strength – the Lord Jesus was crucified in weakness (2 Corinthians 13:4). He could say, "I am poured out like water... My strength is dried up like a potsherd... Thou hast brought Me into the dust of death" (Psalm 22:14-15). Here, again, is the answer to Calvary!

This song of the redeemed is addressed not simply to the Lamb, as was the song of all creation, but rather to "the Lamb that was slain". Throughout eternity, the wounds inflicted at Calvary, and in Pilate's judgment hall, will be a constant reminder of the cost of our redemption. Samuel Rutherford expressed it so aptly,

> *The bride eyes not her garment,*
> *But her dear Bridegroom's face.*
> *I shall not gaze at glory*
> *But on my King of grace,*
> *Not at the crown He gifteth*
> *But on His pierced hand.*
> *The Lamb is all the glory*
> *Of Immanuel's land.*

Surely heaven will reverberate with songs of worship, adoration and praise to the triune God, Father, Son and Holy Spirit. Then there will be an eternal answer to the Lamb who

> "*By weakness and defeat*
> *Won the meed and crown,*

INTRODUCTION

> *Trod all our foes beneath His feet*
> *By being trodden down."*

Then will the chorus go up to the Lamb that was slain:

> *"Worthy!" we cry again,*
> *"Worthy for evermore!"*
> *And at Thy feet, O Lamb once slain,*
> *We worship, we adore.*

JOHN'S VISION

In the opening verses of the vision, given to John in his cell so long ago, there is much to encourage the Christian today. There are eight such themes.

PROMISES

The first of the divine promises in this book is: "Blessed is he that readeth, and they that hear the words of this prophecy, and keep those things which are written therein: for the time is at hand" (1:3). This beatitude is the first of seven to be found in this last book of divine revelation (1:3; 14:13; 16:15; 19:9; 20:6; 22:7,14). In passing, it is interesting to note the similarity between the fourth beatitude in this book and the fourth in the sermon on the mount. "Blessed are they which hunger and thirst after righteousness: for they shall be filled... Blessed are they which are called unto the marriage supper of the Lamb" (Matthew 5:6; Revelation 19:9).

PRONOUNCEMENT

Verse 4 pronounces the blessings which have come to us through God's love: "Grace be unto you, and peace". Grace is the amazing concept of the New Covenant whilst peace is a grand theme of the Old. They are here combined to shed their blessing on the believer's pathway through life. In the book of Deuteronomy, there is a

Hebrew expression, "Shalom, Shalom", which the translators have rendered "perfect peace". What a stark contrast to what the world, with all its materialism, can offer!

How often in Sunday School days we have sung:

> *Oh, the love that drew salvation's plan!*
> *Oh, the grace that brought it down to man!*
> *Oh, the mighty gulf that God did span at Calvary!*
> *Mercy there was great, and grace was free;*
> *Pardon there was multiplied to me;*
> *There my burdened soul found liberty, at Calvary.*

PREDICTION

In verse 7, there is a prediction of the coming King: "Behold, he cometh with clouds; and every eye shall see him, and they also which pierced him: and all kindreds of the earth shall wail because of him. Even so, Amen." This verse surely contains the theme text of the whole of this book of Revelation. His coming will bring joy or fear depending upon one's relationship with the King. For the believer, it will be complete exultation:

> *Oh! The joy to see Thee reigning,*
> *Thee, my own beloved Lord.*
> *Every tongue Thy name confessing,*
> *Worship, honour, glory, blessing,*
> *Brought to Thee with one accord —*
> *Thee, my Master and my Friend,*
> *Vindicated and enthroned,*
> *Unto earth's remotest end*
> *Glorified, adored, and owned!*

PROCLAMATION

The greatness of the Lord is proclaimed in verse 8: "I am Alpha and Omega, the beginning and the ending, saith

INTRODUCTION

the Lord, which is, and which was, and which is to come, the Almighty." Here is the bedrock of our faith. Jesus Christ is the same yesterday, and today, and forever (Hebrews 13:8). He has the preeminence – the Alpha and the Omega. He is the mighty Saviour who not only encapsulates the entire gamut of history, but spans the whole of eternity.

The Hebrew word for 'truth' has but three letters: Aleph, Mem and Tet. These are the first, middle and last letters of the Hebrew alphabet. The rabbis of old equated this word with God – emet, truth – spanning the entire alphabet. In the beginning…God. He who is and who was and who is to come, the Almighty.

PROFFER

Next, we are proffered an example to follow. John is facing a new chapter in the story of his long life. He calls himself a "companion in tribulation… in the kingdom and patience of Jesus Christ… in the isle called Patmos for the word of God, and for the testimony of Jesus Christ" (verse 9). C.H. Mackintosh comments: "Nothing can possibly make up for the lack of secret communion with God, or the training and discipline of His school. The man whom God will use must be endued with such qualifications as can alone be found in the deep and hallowed retirement of the Lord's presence. All God's servants have been made to know and experience the truth of these statements. Moses at Horeb, Elijah at Cherith, Ezekiel at Chebar, Paul in Arabia, and John at Patmos, are all striking examples of the immense practical importance of being alone with God. Moses learned something in 'the backside of the desert' which Egypt's schools could never have taught him. Paul learned more in Arabia than ever he had learned at the feet of Gamaliel. None can teach like God; and all who will learn of Him must be alone with Him. 'In the desert God will teach thee.' Everything is set aside save the stillness and light of the divine Presence. God's voice alone is heard, His light enjoyed, His thoughts received. This is the place to which all must go to be educated for the ministry; and there all must remain if they would succeed in that ministry. In order to act *for* God outside, I should be *with* Him inside. I must be in the secret sanctuary of His presence, else I shall utterly fail. It is when we begin, continue, and end our work at the Master's feet that our service will be of the right kind. It is salutary for us to remember that there is something more than mere doing necessary on the part of the true servant."

PRESCRIPTION

Verse 10 gives us the prescription for victory in the Christian life: "I was in the Spirit on the Lord's day". "Be filled with the Spirit," exclaims Paul to the Ephesians (5:18). It is that complete surrender to the Holy Spirit which enables the believer to realise the potential that God has intended. This is not an overnight phenomenon, although ideally it should be. In practice, this filling, this surrender, is more likely to take place over a period of time, sometimes years. It occurs as one compartment of life after another is opened up to the freedom of the Holy Spirit.

Some years ago, a book entitled 'They found the secret' was published. In it, the lives and ministries of 20 well known Christians were reviewed. It was shown clearly that each one had experienced, at a particular point in their ministry, a confrontation, leading to a surrender to the Holy Spirit which transformed their ministry. Hudson Taylor described this as 'the exchanged life'.

INTRODUCTION

John was in the Spirit on the Lord's day. We should not be complacent with anything but the very best which God has intended for His children. It is this which brings intense joy and victory on our earthly pilgrimage.

PROVISION

Now, here in verse 11, we are introduced to the seven churches of Asia. This is a subject which provides us with so many challenges, both in our personal life, as well as in our church life. Here is a veritable plumb line for the new millennium!

In the succeeding messages to these seven churches, divine warnings and divine commendations are clearly enunciated. The messages to these churches can be interpreted in three ways;

historically — a glimpse of the church situation in the first century.

prophetically — a panoramic view of church history down through the centuries right up to the present time.

topically — providing us with a mirror reflecting the spiritual condition of church life as we move into the 21st century.

The letters to the seven churches will be discussed later and in greater detail.

PRESENTATION

How glorious, and how awesome, is the presentation of Christ in verse 13. Here, John relates his vision of the majesty of Christ. In John's memory would have been the brief revelation which he had shared with Peter and James on the holy Mount when they had seen Christ transfigured before them. This was to be followed, so shortly after, by the scene at Calvary, when the Lord's visage was so marred more than any man's.

But now, before his eyes, he is privileged to have a truly glorious vision of his Lord in divine splendour. He sees Him dressed in a long robe, speaking of judicial authority, and a belt of gold. This latter is not in the usual position around the waist, but rather around the breast, showing that He has completed His work, the work of redemption. "It is finished", was His victorious cry from the cross.

John shares with us in graphic detail the revelation which unfolds before his wondering eyes, the outcome of which causes him to fall "at his feet as dead". He sees One like the Son of Man, standing in the middle of seven golden lamp stands. Seven glorious attributes of His divine majesty can be distinguished.

WISDOM

His head and His hair were white with the whiteness of wool, like snow. Here was displayed His purity and His eternal deity. It is surely also a portrait which displays wisdom. So Daniel, centuries earlier, could write, "I beheld...the Ancient of days...whose garment was white as snow, and the hair of his head like the pure wool" (7:9). Great is the Lord and greatly to be praised (Psalm 48:1)!

WATCHFULNESS

His eyes were like a burning flame – piercing, penetrating, searching. Peter experienced those eyes when, having denied his Lord, those eyes turned upon him. They melted Peter and he went out into the night weeping bitterly. Who can? Who will? – in that coming day be able to withstand the piercing eyes of the Judge of all the earth? But "now is the accepted time; behold, now is the day of salvation" (2 Corinthians 6:2).

INTRODUCTION

WALK

His feet were like burnished bronze when it has been refined in a furnace. Isaiah could look on to a day when the Lord would say, "I have trodden the winepress alone" (63:3). So John, later in his vision, would see the Lord as the One who "treadeth the winepress of the fierceness and wrath of Almighty God" (19:15). We are reminded of the famous, solemn lines of Julia Ward Howe:

> *Mine eyes have seen the glory of the coming of the Lord;*
> *He is trampling out the vintage where the grapes of wrath are stored.*
> *He hath loosed the fateful lightning of His terrible swift sword.*
> *Our God is marching on.*

WARMTH

We read that His voice was like the sound of many waters. There is a great warmth in this expression. It denotes the quiet majesty of the ocean in its depth and resonance. Breaking in music upon the sands of time, John hears Him say, "Fear not; I am the first and the last" (verse 17). Surely, as we read these verses, we too can hear the sound of the Aegean and its warmth as it laps the shores of this little island.

WORTHINESS

"And he had in his right hand seven stars" (verse 16). He alone is worthy to hold the seven stars. He alone is worthy to take the scroll from Him who sat on the throne, and to open the seals (5:9).

We remember that God hath made this same Jesus both Lord and Christ. "O sing unto the LORD a new song; for he hath done marvellous things: his right hand and his holy arm hath gotten him the victory" (Psalm 98:1). Yes…He is worthy!

WORD

Out of His mouth came a two edged sword, figurative of the word of God (Ephesians 6:17). Here is a timely reminder of the holiness of the Lord. He is seen in awesome majesty. He upholds all things by the word of His power (Hebrews 1:3).

To the child of God, redeemed by His precious blood, He is the Beloved, the heavenly Bridegroom. But to those who have rejected and spurned His love and overtures of mercy during this day of grace, He is the Judge – the One before whose face heaven and earth flee away. May we respond now, in this day of grace, to His gracious words, "Come unto me, all ye that labour and are heavy laden, and I will give you rest" (Matthew 11:28).

WORSHIP

Little wonder that, as John has this vision of Christ in majesty, he falls at His feet! His face was shining like the sun in all its brilliance. No longer was His face marred. No longer can it be said that He hath no form or comeliness (Isaiah 53:2).

By faith we, too, see Jesus crowned with glory and honour (Hebrews 2:9). So we, too, bow in worship. He, who was made a little lower than the angels for the suffering of death, is now the subject and the object of our worship and adoration. What will it be when faith gives place to sight, and we see Him face to face, with "no darkling veil between"?!

To see Thee face to face,
Thy perfect likeness wear,

INTRODUCTION

And all Thy ways of wondrous grace
Through endless years declare!

These words of Sir Edward Denny, so often sung around the Lord's Table while partaking of the bread and wine, remind us ever again of the mighty sacrifice of Calvary.

How fitting are the words which immediately precede this book of the Revelation:

> "Now unto him that is able to keep you from falling, and to present you faultless before the presence of his glory with exceeding joy, to the only wise God our Saviour, be glory and majesty, dominion and power, both now and ever. Amen" (Jude 24,25).

2. The Letters to the Seven Churches

INTRODUCTION

Chapters 2 and 3 of the Revelation detail the letters sent from God to the seven churches situated in what is today the country of Turkey. In chapter 1, we saw that the messages to these churches can be interpreted in three ways:

historically – giving us a glimpse of the church situation in the 1st century.

prophetically – giving us a panoramic view of church history down through the centuries right up to the present time.

topically – providing us with a mirror reflecting the spiritual condition of church life as we move into the 21st century.

The historic interpretation scarcely requires further comment. It will be convenient to examine the prophetic interpretation in more detail. Lessons for our 21st century will be drawn as appropriate to each church. The prophetic interpretation can be summarised as follows:

THE LETTERS TO THE SEVEN CHURCHES

Ephesus   *The Apostolic Church*   (Pentecost to AD 70)
Smyrna   *The Martyr Church*   (AD 70 to AD 312)
Pergamum   *The State Church*   (AD 312 to AD 606)
Thyatira   *The Established Church*   (AD 606 to AD 1520)
Sardis   *The Reformation Church*   (AD 1520 to AD 1750)
Philadelphia   *The Missionary Church*   (AD 1750 to AD 1900)
Laodicea   *The Apostate Church*   (from AD 1900 to the Rapture).

An interesting, although by no means a generally accepted, interpretation is to use the Kingdom parables of Matthew 13 as an overview of the history of these churches. Interestingly, there are seven parables in Matthew 13. The first four are told to the multitudes by the seaside, to 'men of sight' (verses 1,2). These show comparative failure and can be identified with the first four churches:

The Sower   – only 25% of the seed fruitful (Ephesus)
The Darnel   – the Enemy at work sowing false seed, so very like wheat (Smyrna)
The Mustard Seed   – unnatural growth and false development (Pergamum)
The Leaven (Yeast)   – compromise marring witness (Thyatira).

These reveal the processes of the Kingdom through this age as seen on the human level.

The final three parables are told in the house to Jesus' disciples, to 'men of faith'.

The Treasure   – purchased by the Redeemer's blood (Sardis)
The Pearl   – formed through suffering (Philadelphia)

The Dragnet — consummation of the age and angel activity (Laodicea).

These three reveal the processes of the Kingdom from the divine viewpoint – the divine purpose and standard.

The locations of the churches themselves can still be identified. Three are living and dynamic cities today: Smyrna (Izmir); Philadelphia (Alasenia); Thyatira (Akhisar). The remaining four are archaeological sites and can be visited. Ephesus is the most impressive site of the four.

Come with me now to the Seven Churches!

3. Ephesus

Ephesus was one of the great cities of the ancient world. In the days of Paul, it was a beautiful city, right by the sea. Within its boundaries was one of the seven wonders of the ancient world – the temple of the goddess Diana (Artemis), perhaps the most famous building in the world at that time. Sadly, today, there is hardly a stone left to commemorate it.

Here, too, is the great theatre to which Paul's travelling companions, Gaius and Aristarchus, were dragged by the Ephesian mob (Acts 19:29). Standing there today, one can almost hear their frenzied shouts, "Great is Diana of the Ephesians". But now all is silent; everything is in ruins. The city was destroyed in AD 262. Before its destruction, Ephesus was a wealthy city and highly cultured, but corruption gradually took its toll.

Against this background, the infant church at Ephesus was truly remarkable. Surrounded by paganism and ancient mythology and superstition, it nevertheless developed a heightened sense of worship and a deep understanding of the new 'religion' introduced by Paul. Only to such a church could Paul unfold the deep truths of his epistle to the Ephesians.

However, as the years passed by, beneath the surface all was not well. To the outsider, things might seem outwardly fine. Here would seem to be a thriving, busy assembly, one which had attained great spiritual heights. It should be pointed out, and it is salutary to note, that the letter we are considering in Revelation 2 was written only 35 years after the one sent by Paul to that same church.

Here was a church which had enjoyed such a morning of promise, their early zeal exemplified by the burning of 3,000 books on sorcery! Here was displayed a movement of power, a lighthouse in a sea of paganism. It had become a vast mission field in a world of darkness.

The apostle John, himself, had lived there and, according to tradition, would yet again once his exile was over. Mary, the mother of our Lord, had also resided there. This church was waging a great spiritual battle and certainly needed the whole armour of God, as detailed in Ephesians 6. Their driving force received a seven-fold commendation for their work, labour and patience (Revelation 2:2,3). Never was a church organisation so complete!

BUT...there was a missing ingredient!! This would lead to their downfall and demise. They not only lacked love but, of far greater significance, *they had left their first love – their bridal love*. This is a love which defies analysis. It is a love which means abandonment of all for a love which has abandoned all.

Ruin or renewal was the stark choice. Failure meant the removal of the lampstand, the loss of testimony. Sadly, failure came. The lampstand was removed and the rest, as it is said, is history. That failure is witnessed by all who travel to Turkey today and stand amongst the ruins of that once great city.

First love for Jesus is the essential prerequisite for a fulfilling Christian life. In this letter, the divine finger is pointed at the whole assembly. So today, each church fellowship must take note of this vital lesson. The words of the Lord Jesus still challenge us, "By this shall all men know that ye are my disciples, if ye have love one to another" (John 13:35).

This first love must be the hallmark of each assembly. However, it is equally important for the individual believer. First love for Jesus is paramount. "Though I speak with the tongues of men and of angels, but have not love, I have become as sounding brass or a clanging cymbal" (1 Corinthians 13:1). "Without first love we may retain ceaseless activity, immaculate purity, severest orthodoxy, but there will be no light shining in a dark place. It is not our doing that lightens the world. It is not our ceremonial cleanness that helps men. It is not our correctness in the holding of truth that helps a dying race. It is our love first for our Master, then for each other, and then for the world" (G. Campbell Morgan).

When danger signals flash, and warning signs become evident, the call from heaven remains ever the same – REPENT. In repentance, we can rediscover the joy of communion and the love of Christ. Then we might take up the words of M. Basilea Schlink:

> *O none can be loved as is Jesus.*
> *None like Him is found anywhere.*

*'Tis He whom I love, whom I live for,
For no one with Him can compare.*

*So all that I have I will give Him;
I'll sacrifice all I hold dear.
My whole life to Jesus belonging,
My heart seeks my Lord to revere.*

*I follow now close in His footsteps
The path that He trod here below.
I only desire what He gives me,
And only His way I will go.*

*My heart is at peace and so joyful,
For all I desire He supplies.
I look now for nothing but Jesus,
Who all of my hope satisfies.*

4. Smyrna

Today, as in Bible times, Smyrna (Izmir) is a thriving and prosperous city. After Istanbul and Ankara, it ranks as the third largest city in Turkey. In the first century, together with most of the early churches, the church in Smyrna faced suffering, slander and poverty. Suffering was, in fact, the chief characteristic of the church at Smyrna. The Lord took particular note of this and gave them this special word of comfort: "Fear none of those things which thou shalt *suffer*…be thou faithful unto *death*, and I will give thee a crown of life" (2:10).

MYRRH

'Smyrna' means 'myrrh'. How telling it is that the main export from Smyrna at that time was indeed myrrh. More than anything else, myrrh symbolises the suffering of the church at Smyrna. The problem of pain and suffering has occupied many minds down through the ages. Christian assurance in the face of such suffering is nowhere better expressed than in the famous, simple lines:

> *Not till the loom is silent,*
> *And the shuttles cease to fly,*
> *Will God unroll the canvas*
> *And explain the reason why*

> *The dark threads were as needful*
> *In the Weaver's skilful hands*
> *As the threads of gold and silver*
> *For the pattern He has planned.*

The children of Israel had not travelled far on their journey through the wilderness before they encountered the bitter water of Marah. In response to their distress, the Lord showed Moses a tree which, when he had cast it into the waters, made the waters sweet (Exodus 15:23-25). Likewise today, when suffering comes and bitterness is experienced, the believer's recourse must always be the cross of Christ. It is there that all bitterness evaporates as Calvary love overrides the pain. The hymn writer, Fanny Crosby, expresses it well:

> *Jesus, keep me near the cross.*
> *There a precious fountain,*
> *Free to all, a healing stream,*
> *Flows from Calvary's mountain.*
> *In the cross, in the cross,*
> *Be my glory ever.*

During much of the period represented by the Smyrna church, the Roman emperors were largely responsible for much of the persecution and suffering. They were Nero (AD 54), Domitian (AD 81), Trajan (AD 98), Septimus Severus (AD 193), Maximin (AD 235), Decius (AD 249), Valerian (AD 254), Aurelian (AD 270) and Diocletian (AD 284).

Perhaps the church's most famous martyr was Polycarp, who was bishop of Smyrna from AD 115-156. The proconsul, Statius Quadratus, tried to make Polycarp, as an old man of 86, deny his faith. He refused, saying, "Eighty and six years have I served Him, and He has done me no ill. How can I then blaspheme my King who hath served me?" Polycarp was then burnt at the stake. The shouts of the enraged crowd, as reported by Eusebius, are perhaps the highest tribute to this faithful martyr: "This is the teacher of Asia, the destroyer of our gods. This is the father of the churches."

This incident gives us a small insight into the heightened tensions of the day. Little wonder, then, that Smyrna is remembered as the suffering church, the martyr church. For those who find themselves in a Smyrna situation today, Psalm 73 provides a bedrock. The final verse of that psalm reads, "But it is good for me to draw near to God: I have put my trust in the Lord God, that I may declare all thy works".

Myrrh was, of course, one of the gifts brought by the wise men, together with frankincense and gold, to the young child, Jesus. It is appropriate, at this stage, to consider the significance of these other gifts in relation to the church at Smyrna.

FRANKINCENSE

Frankincense, with its fragrant odour on burning, is in marked contrast to the bitter perfume of myrrh. Myrrh, as we have seen, speaks to us of suffering. Frankincense would speak of fragrance, or sweetness. David had the assurance that "weeping may endure for a night, but joy cometh in the morning" (Psalms 30:5). With God, suffering is never the end so far as the believer is concerned. The suffering of Good Friday was followed by the triumph of Easter Day!

It is significant that in the Temple worship, the path from the great altar of sacrifice led through to the golden altar of incense. Here, the fragrance of the incense of worship arose to the very throne of heaven.

"Until the day break, and the shadows flee away, I will get me to the mountain of myrrh, and to the hill of frankincense". Thus spoke the bride in the Song of Solomon (4:6). Centuries later, in the shadow of Calvary, Mary of Bethany expressed her love for her Lord by anointing Him with precious ointment of spikenard. The house was filled with the odour of the ointment (John 12:1-3). The hymn writer, Helena von Poseck, catches the spirit of that incident so beautifully,

Thy Name, blessed Lord, is as ointment poured forth,
And e'en as we utter it, fragrance doth rise
To the Father, who only its excellent worth,
Its matchless perfection, in fullness can prize.

Oh, Name of sweet savour, a savour of rest,
The Name of the Victim, the Lamb that was slain!
Oh, Name of God's loved One in whom we are blest!
Oh, Name ever worthy, all homage be given.

GOLD

Resting in Christ, drawing close to Him in worship, we experience first the gold of communion and then, finally, the city of gold. To the suffering believers at Smyrna the Master says, "I know" (2:9). He has suffered to the utmost, and now He presences Himself with His own. Their suffering, also, will but endure for the night. It is limited. "Ten days", He tells the church as they are encouraged to endure (verse 10). Yes! Joy *will* come in the morning.

We wait for that day with ever growing expectation. Until then, however, we have the promise of His presence. In response to the well known hymn, "I need Thee every hour", D.W. Whittle was encouraged to write,

Moment by moment I'm kept in His love.
Moment by moment I've power from above.
Looking to Jesus till glory doth shine,
Moment by moment, O Lord, I am Thine.

So David could write, "Yea, though I walk through the valley of the shadow of death…thou art with me" (Psalm 23:4).

Christ not only promises His comfort and companionship, but also the crown of victory. He reminds those at Smyrna that, though they may be in poverty materially, yet they are rich spiritually. With these resources, they are exhorted to be faithful unto death (verses 9,10). Indeed, this is the martyr church, but suffering saints will reign with Christ! The Lord has Himself gone through shadow and pain. He will lead through tribulation, through death, to life, to crowning and the city of gold.

This letter to Smyrna, like that to Philadelphia, contains no warnings, but only promises. Reviewing the history of this church, we see how well the parable of the wheat and tares (darnel) illustrates their situation. Darnel is so like wheat and is sown by the enemy, reminding us of the Lord's warning, "Beware of false prophets, which come to you in sheep's clothing, but inwardly they are ravening wolves" (Matthew 7:15). Satan had done his utmost to infiltrate the church at Smyrna.

We, today, can be encouraged by this letter. We are living in the end times. Moral and spiritual darkness is intensifying in our world. Evil is on the march as never before in the history of the Church. The driving force of our earthly pilgrimage is the knowledge that soon, and very soon, we shall see the King in His beauty, with no "darkling veil between".

It is fitting to close this meditation with the closing words of Scripture, "Surely I come quickly. Even so, come, Lord Jesus."

5. Pergamum

In the third century BC, Pergamum was the centre of the Attilid kingdom. (The AV 'Pergamos' is better translated 'Pergamum'.) Later, in 133 BC, it was bequeathed to Rome by Attalus the Third. Pergamum was probably the wealthiest of the seven cities of Revelation chapters 2 and 3, and was devoted to wealth and fashion. Unlike Ephesus, however, it was not a commercial centre. The god of medicine was a main object of worship. Indeed, one of its citizens, Dr. Galen, became famous for his teaching and healing methods.

The great altar to Zeus, towering some 800 feet above the surrounding plain, dominated the city, literally and in every way. Its construction began in 180 BC and took 20 years to complete. It was destroyed in the early days of Christianity as it was considered to be the throne of Satan (2:13). Pergamum was the first city in Asia Minor to have a temple dedicated to the Emperor Augustus and Rome. As the capital of the province, it thus became the centre of the imperial cult in the entire region.

The parable of the mustard seed (Matthew 13), is so relevant to the situation which developed in Pergamum following the victories of Constantine. In AD 313,

Constantine decided to legalise Christianity and to make it the religion of his empire. Mustard, of course, is a herb, not a tree. What we have in the parable is abnormal, unnatural growth. This is exactly what we see happening in Pergamum. Constantine's decision resulted in Pergamum becoming a religious centre. Local believers in the city became swamped with professing Christians. Birds of the air (verse 32), were indeed nesting in its branches!

The mustard tree effect still has a telling message for the Church today. True Christians and those who are Christians only in name, possessors and professors, mingle in many congregations and, as we see in the parable of the wise and foolish virgins (Matthew 25), there is often little outward sign to distinguish them. The need for the Church militant is to remain true to its calling in purity and holiness. This is all the more necessary in an age of increasing liberalism and the strident calls for toleration.

> *Keep me true, Lord Jesus, keep me true!*
> *Keep me true, Lord Jesus, keep me true!*
> *There's a race that I must run,*
> *There are victories to be won;*
> *Give me power, every hour, to be true!*

The church at Pergamum found itself in the midst of an alien, hostile world, as Christians do today. What is its message for today? It will be convenient to consider this under three headings.

The World – My Parish

So exclaimed John Wesley! How right he was to lift up his eyes to see the vast harvest field (John 4:35). In our desire to unite in this global battle, we must be able to recognise the inherent dangers of ecumenism. The enemy is hard at work in the world Church making it all the more imperative for the Body of Christ to follow the 'Daniel concept' to maintain spiritual separation from all that seeks to defile. We must stand firm and oppose, with all the vigour we can muster, the widely held belief that there are many roads leading to God. Be warned! In the 'mustard tree' situation, heresy creeps in by stealth.

Scripture is emphatic that there is only one way, and that a narrow way. Jesus, who could welcome all to come to Him (Matthew 11:28), nevertheless insisted, "I am the way…no man cometh unto the Father, but by me" (John 14:6). Let us plainly declare with Paul: "God forbid that I should glory, save in the cross of our Lord Jesus Christ, by whom the world is crucified unto me, and I unto the world. For in Christ Jesus neither circumcision availeth anything, nor uncircumcision, but a new creature" (Galatians 6:14,15).

THE WORLD – MY PERIL

Two key issues faced the church in Pergamum in those initial days of the 'State Church': collaboration and compromise. The challenge is just as great today! We have the New Age movement seeking to appear as an angel of light, with its general philosophy of self-sufficiency: "man can save himself". This is in total contradiction to essential Christian doctrine. New Age points to a coming Messiah who will help to build a new world, based on global power, global control, and global worship.

The situation of the church at Pergamum highlights the peril of entering into alliance with forces under the control of Satan. It is the philosophy which hinges on the doctrine of Balaam: compromise under pagan pressures. The Church in this situation is in very real danger of losing its pilgrim character and heading towards world conformity.

New Age, new conflicts – these present new challenges to the present day Church. The warning signs are clear. The message once again is that of repentance: "Repent; or else I will come unto thee quickly" (verse 16), together with a call to join the ranks of the overcomers to whom glorious promises are given: "To him that overcometh will I give to eat of the hidden manna, and will give him a white stone, and in the stone a new name written, which no man knoweth saving he that receiveth it" (verse 17).

We are not alone in this vital battle of Faith: "seeing we… are compassed about with so great a cloud of witnesses, let us lay aside every weight, and the sin which doth so easily beset us, and let us run with patience the race that is set before us, *looking unto Jesus*" (Hebrews 12:1,2).

> *Oh, let me feel Thee near me;*
> *The world is ever near;*
> *I see the sights that dazzle,*
> *The tempting sounds I hear.*
> *My foes are ever near me,*
> *Around me and within;*
> *But, Jesus, draw Thou nearer*
> *And shield my soul from sin.*
>
> *O Jesus, Thou hast promised*
> *To all who follow Thee*
> *That where Thou art in glory*
> *There shall Thy servant be;*
> *And, Jesus, I have promised*
> *To serve Thee to the end.*

> *Oh, give me grace to follow*
> *My Master and my Friend.*

The World – My Past

"The world behind me, the cross before me, no turning back, no turning back." The Pergamum situation calls for such a song of resolve. The world had engulfed the church at Pergamum. The ability to overcome called for present day Daniels then, as it still calls today.

The world we face today is similar to that which Pergamum faced. It is a world which presents a complete grey area where the positives and negatives are so blurred that the dividing line is completely smudged. In one part of the world, we even have a situation where, should a car driver ignore a red traffic light and by so doing hits another car which is legitimately crossing on the green light, both drivers are held equally to blame! The argument is that if the 'correct' driver had not been there, no accident would have occurred!

In today's world, it is absolutely imperative for the Christian not only to stand firm, but also to make perfectly clear where he, or she, stands.

> *Dare to be a Daniel!*
> *Dare to stand alone!*
> *Dare to have a purpose firm!*
> *Dare to make it known!*

Such boldness cannot be achieved without divine strength. Through the grace of God, we have access to hidden resources. "I can", said Paul, "do all things through Christ which strengtheneth me" (Philippians 4:13). The old adage is still true: Satan trembles when he sees the weakest saint upon his knees!

The Church of Jesus Christ must not tolerate within her borders those who lower the standard of truth's requirements. As once stated, "The key to the future is not held in the hands of conspiring sinful men or the prince of hell." Only God and His Christ hold the key to the future of the world and the destiny of mankind. Jesus is coming! The crown is His! Yes! No turning back, no compromise!

The call still comes to us today:

> *Rise, my soul, thy God directs thee,*
> *Stranger hands no more impede;*
> *Pass thou on, His hand protects thee,*
> *Strength that has the captive freed.*
>
> *Light divine surrounds thy going,*
> *God Himself shall mark thy way;*
> *Secret blessings, richly flowing,*
> *Lead to everlasting day.*

(J.N.Darby)

6. Thyatira

Present day Thyatira, or Akhisar as it is now called, is a thriving modern city. In the 1st century AD, it was relatively unimportant, possibly the least important of the seven cities. It was, however, an important outpost for the protection of Pergamum and Sardis, two of the world's greatest capitals at different times.

It was a town of merchants and craftsmen, with a wide variety of guilds. Guild meetings included a common meal dedicated to a pagan deity. Such meetings frequently ended in debauchery. The Christians at Thyatira clearly could not associate themselves with these activities while, at the same time, maintaining their faith. Amongst its many trades were dyeing, clothing and brass-working. It might even have been through the witness of Lydia, a seller of the locally produced dye (Acts 16:14), that these early Christians had come to faith.

In Pergamum, as we saw, the church faced the challenge of unnatural development, as revealed in the parable of the mustard seed (Matthew 13). The church at Thyatira faced yet another challenge, a challenge which is revealed in the parable of the yeast. The church was being infiltrated by enemies of the cross. This was an inner evil, permeating the whole fellowship. In such circumstances, it is essential for the body of Christ to close ranks and for its individual members to be on their guard. Three basic ingredients become highlighted: personal faith; personal fidelity; personal future.

Personal Faith

The Inner Power

In the Thyatiran situation, then as now, the individual believer has to be aware of the pervading evil and then to experience the inner power of God to combat it. On a voyage across the Atlantic, a friend of the ship's captain was invited on to the bridge. The liner encountered a heavy storm, greatly alarming the passenger. He glanced anxiously at his friend, the captain, but noticed that the captain looked completely relaxed and calm. "Aren't you afraid?" he shouted, trying to make himself heard above the fury of the storm. Without a word, the captain handed his friend the bridge telephone. Clamping it to his ear, the noise of the storm was silenced. All he could hear was the powerful throb of the mighty turbines, way down in the bowels of the great ship. Then he understood!

The Christian, too, can access inner power, power to withstand the storm of surrounding evil.

> *Power, to conquer every subtle foe.*
> *Power, to bid the alluring tempter go.*
> *Power, to make this world a heaven below*
> *In Christ for me.*

Such power is accessed in the secret of His presence. The writer of the letter to the Hebrews exhorts the worshipper to pass through the veil (Hebrews 10:19-25). The blood-sprinkled mercy seat is there. How precious this is to the child of God! What a privilege to be able to draw aside in the quietness of communion! Such communion was experienced by Paul Gerhardt, at a time of great stress:

> *Through waves and clouds and storms*
> *His power will clear thy way.*
> *Wait thou His time; the darkest night*
> *Shall end in brightest day.*
>
> *Leave to His sovereign sway*
> *To choose and to command;*
> *So shalt thou, wondering, own His way,*
> *How wise, how strong, His hand.*

With this inner power, we can proclaim with Paul, "I can do all things through Christ which strengtheneth me" (Philippians 4:13).

THE OUTWARD EXPRESSION

Inner power may have to be martialled to confront the outward expression presented by the church. From an outsider's point of view, all might have seemed well in the church at Thyatira. The Lord could note their love, their faith, their patience, and their works (2:19). There would appear to be progress and development. The church would appear to have a better track record than that at Ephesus. Outwardly fine, but the yeast effect was insidious, quietly working in the inner recesses of assembly life. This situation, sadly, is not unknown today! In such a situation, the child of God needs a stiff, spiritual backbone as well as the courage to speak out against the liberal toleration of false teaching being introduced and which is being accepted by the majority.

THE ONWARD WALK

As the church progresses, we note that there is spiritual sensitivity on the one hand whilst, at the same time, there are those who are pressing on regardless, quite oblivious to the real state of things. However, danger signals are flashing. The Son of God Himself is examining the situation. His penetrating eyes, likened to a flame of fire, are piercing through the veneer of spirituality (verse 18). The Lord, in His review of the church at Thyatira, tells them that, despite the good points, He has a few things against them (verse 20). At the same time, a special appeal is made to the faithful members in the congregation (verse 24).

Personal Fidelity

Yes, the Thyatiran situation calls not only for personal faith, but also for personal fidelity with which to face hostility, to fight the invading cancer, to have the courage to stand against the evil which threatens to engulf the church. This was a church which had accepted Jezebel (verse 20) and the teaching she promulgated. Jezebel represented everything that was unscrupulous: evil teaching, evil practices, both representing the deep things of Satan.

It is said that if you drop a frog into a saucepan of boiling water, it will jump straight out again. However, if you place the frog into a pan of cold water and gently heat it, you will cook it! It will not have realised the danger it was in, until too late. This is a true picture of Thyatira, as it is of the church today. If our saintly forbears were to return today, they would jump straight out again – shocked by prevailing moral and spiritual conditions, shocked to see a tolerant and silent church. As it is, the cooking process continues. Is it already too late for the true church to wake up and to raise its voice in protest and call for national repentance?

Personal Future

Holding Fast

The call comes loud and clear – to hold fast with absolute loyalty to Christ. No further burden will be put upon those remaining loyal (verses 24,25).

Heralding the Dawn

Then comes the promise: "I will give him the morning star" (verse 28). Sorrows may endure for a night, but dayspring is at hand (2 Peter 1:19). Here is a glorious promise – the herald of a new day, the harbinger of the day of glory.

Such a promise should completely transform the outlook of each believer. No compromise will be tolerated; his light will shine out in the deepening darkness, just as spelt out in the Sunday School chorus:

> *Keep me shining, Lord,*
> *Keep me shining, Lord,*
> *In all I say and do*
> *That the world may see*
> *Christ lives in me*
> *And learn to love Him too.*

It is virtually impossible adequately to describe the sight that lifts one's spirit when, after a long, dark night in the desert, the morning star appears in the heavens. Here, at last, is the sure sign that the night is passing and that soon, very soon, the sun will rise into a cloudless sky in royal splendour.

In a land-locked African village at the foot of a tall mountain, three boys received a challenge. A prize was to be offered to the boy who could climb to the highest point. Each had to exhibit proof of his achievement. After a short interval, the first boy returned. In his hand was a plant which could only grow above a certain altitude. Presently, the second boy arrived. He, too, had a plant which could only grow at a somewhat higher altitude. After a long absence, the third boy ran into the village. There was no plant in his hand but his eyes shone with a look which beggared description. His eyes were ablaze with wonder. He called out, "I saw the sea. I saw the sea." Never before had he seen the mighty ocean. Now from the mountain peak he had, for the first time, beheld the majesty of the mighty waves!

"Ye are the light of the world," said the Lord Jesus. "Let your light so shine" (Matthew 5:14,16). Yes, even in this world, the world of compromise, the world of toleration, the world of Thyatira! Let the glorious hope shine out in a dark world! Above all…hold fast!

7. Sardis

At the time this letter was addressed to the church in Sardis, Sardis was already a city of past glories. It was once the capital of the Lydian kingdom and achieved its greatest fame under Croesus in the 6th century BC. Gradually, it sank into relative obscurity though it was still a centre for commerce, mainly for woollen goods and particularly in the art of dyeing wool.

The church in Sardis presented a veneer of spirituality, but in reality it was dead. Amongst its number, there were indeed a few true believers. In the interpretation of the parables of Matthew 13 suggested in chapter 2, Sardis is represented by the buried treasure (verse 44). In this parable, the field speaks to us of the world, a world in rebellion against God, a world under the heel of the prince of this world. Within this world, however, there is a treasure – those who have been purchased by the precious blood of the Lamb. To the surrounding professing church, the Lord says, "Thou hast a name that thou livest, and art dead" (Revelation 3:1).

In considering the Sardis situation, three things stand out: condemnation, confrontation, commendation.

CONDEMNATION

OUTWARD MANIFESTATION

The first noticeable factor is that, in this letter, condemnation rather than commendation comes first. No doubt it was a busy church, full of activity, full of works. Externally all seemed normal. Here was a live church by all accounts, well organised and outwardly very difficult to fault.

INWARD MORTIFICATION

Walking down the steep pathway which leads from the top of the Mount of Olives to Gethsemane, we see large areas of whitened sepulchres. These vividly remind us of the Lord's outspoken accusation: "Woe unto you, scribes and Pharisees, hypocrites! For ye are like unto whitened sepulchres, which indeed appear beautiful outward, but are within full of dead men's bones, and of all uncleanness" (Matthew 23:27).

Sardis was probably the most picturesquely situated of all the seven churches. Sadly, here was a church in beautiful surroundings, outwardly lovely, but mortification had already set in. It was but a beautifully adorned corpse!

ONWARD MORIBUND

There was nothing in Sardis, nothing at all, which could satisfy the heart of Christ. There was no fulfilment of their early promise. Their onward march only produced further condemnation.

What a tragic picture unfolds before our eyes. This was a company who had taken their place as Christians, performing all the outward manifestations of Christians – yet without life, without relationship with the Life-giver. There was no experience here of the abundant life which the Lord promises to His own. The death of this church stands in stark contrast to the death of the believer to the world around. The believer is dead to the world but alive unto God!

> *His dying crimson, like a robe*
> *Spread o'er His body on the tree.*
> *Then am I dead to all the globe*
> *And all the globe is dead to me.*

Sardis was just the opposite of this. Here we see a church of early promise but, by not having its eyes on the Lord, it becomes moribund. The terrible consequence is the removal of the lampstand and a church which disappears into history.

How thankful we should be that the Holy Spirit has seen fit to bring these early churches to our attention. May it not be true of us, as expressed in Winston Churchill's celebrated dictum: "What we learn from history is that we don't learn from history"!

CONFRONTATION

ADVENT TO BE

"I will come", said the Lord (verse 3), surely reminding them of the teaching they had received. "As a thief in the night"…yes, in the twinkling of an eye.

> *It may be at morn, when the day is awaking,*
> *When sunlight through darkness and shadow is breaking,*
> *That Jesus will come in the fullness of glory*
> *To receive from the world His own.*

What a glorious promise this is! But oh, how different is such a promise when other circumstances prevail. When sacred things lose their power, precious things lose their blessedness.

The sun can have two effects. It can warm and heal, or it can scorch. To the child of God, the coming of the Saviour is a subject of intense joy and of joyful anticipation. To the professing Christian, to the world at large, it spells terror. They will have to face the subsequent wrath of the Lamb. Beloved Christian, may we not be ashamed at His coming, but rather be the happy recipients of His commendation, "Well done, good and faithful servant, enter thou into the joy of thy Lord".

Assessment Will Be

The second coming of Christ will be fulfilled in two stages. Firstly, the Lord will return for His church, all those who have been redeemed by His blood. This event will not be witnessed by the world. It is a secret rapture. Secondly, the Lord will return to earth surrounded by a heavenly host, and by the redeemed. His feet will touch the Mount of Olives, and He will return in triumph to His city, Jerusalem, as King of kings and Lord of lords.

> *I cannot tell how all the lands shall worship,*
> *When at His bidding, every storm is stilled,*
> *Or who can say how great the jubilation*
> *When all the hearts of men with love are filled.*

> *But this I know, the skies will fill with rapture,*
> *And myriad, myriad human voices sing,*
> *And earth to heaven, and heaven to earth will answer,*
> *At last the Saviour, Saviour of the world, is King.*

This glorious reign of the Messiah will usher in the millennium – a thousand years of peace. Then will all the nations recognise His sovereignty. At that time, a valley will be opened up. In that valley, the valley of Jehoshaphat, the Lord will sit as judge of the nations.

Adjudication Soon To Be

Following this judgment and the thousand years of peace, there will follow the great resurrection of all those who, down through the centuries, have died in unbelief. This is the judgment of the Great White Throne, when the dead, small and great, are arrayed before the Judge. Yes! Assessment there will be, and adjudication will follow, as the books are opened and the deeds of all will be made manifest. How relevant, therefore, is the message to Sardis, a message which comes in force to us today, "Hold fast, and repent" (verse 3). Sardis is a true picture of dead orthodoxy and stands as a timely warning to all dead churches today.

Commendation

Three features stand out:

1. clothed in white raiment
2. codified in the Book of Life
3. confessed before the Father and His angels.

Here is the other side of the picture. Even in the dead church, there is buried treasure – those who are overcomers. Wonderful promises are given to these. They will be clothed with the dress of heaven. Their names will not be blotted out of the Book of Life. Their names will be confessed by the Lord before the Father and His angels (verses 4,5). The call to the overcomer still sounds today: "Be watchful, and strengthen the things that remain" (verse 2).

Sardis, together with the ruins of Capernaum, Bethsaida and Chorazin serve as powerful warning signs to us today of the fate of those who, though having been blessed by God, have rejected His overtures. Therefore, "Let *us* lay aside every weight, and the sin which doth so easily beset *us*, and let *us* run with patience the race that is set before *us*, looking unto Jesus the author and finisher of our faith" (Hebrews 12:1,2).

8. Philadelphia

Philadelphia, the city of brotherly love as its name implies, was the least important city of the seven. Its name today is Alasehir, but its former name came from Attalus the Second of Pergamum. He was given the name Philadelphus because of his love for his brother who had preceded him as king. The city was founded during his reign in the second century BC, as an outpost of Pergamum. Even then it was a missionary city!

The church in Philadelphia, together with that of Smyrna, were the only two churches not to receive any condemnations.

THE MISSIONARY CHALLENGE

THE OPEN DOOR

Philadelphia was strategically placed – on the outer edge of Hellenistic civilisation. Here, by reason of its location, it could 'broadcast' the transforming power of the Gospel. Despite the surrounding hatred and the opposition to this new faith, a faith which threatened to overthrow pagan worship, the Lord had presented them with this challenge of an open door (3:7).

The Lord Jesus is the same yesterday, today and for ever. He continues to present His church with open doors. Let us recognise these openings and press forward to make Christ known. The Lord knows that we have little strength, but:

> *Be valiant, be strong, resist the powers of sin!*
> *The fight is long, the foe is strong, but you shall win;*
> *For the power of Christ — the Stronger than the strong —*
> *You shall be more than conqueror.*
> *Be valiant, be strong!*

The Obedient Disciple

The key note is obedience. The command is to go into all the world and disciple all nations. The church which has lost its missionary zeal is a dying church. There is a world to be won – a world which is on our own doorstep. In facing this task, the most important factor is loyalty to Jesus and the knowledge that the battle is not ours, but His! He will provide the resources.

Despite the innumerable difficulties in reaching a lost world, every available means should be harnessed, including radio, television, and all aspects of information technology. The message is unchanging, but the method of proclaiming it will always need to be brought up to date. We no longer live in the magic lantern age!

The Omnipotent Deliverer

Only when launching out into a programme of outreach will we fully realise how utterly dependent we are on the power of God. To the church at Philadelphia came the assurance, "I will keep thee" (verse 10). We need to cling to promises such as these today. The Lord is our rock, our fortress, our deliverer.

The vision which the servant of Elisha had at Dothan is as much a reality today as it was then (2 Kings 6:17). It is not for nothing that our God is called Jehovah Sabaoth – the Lord of armies.

> *"We rest on Thee" — our shield and our defender!*
> *We go not forth alone against the foe;*
> *Strong in Thy strength, safe in Thy keeping tender,*
> *"We rest on Thee, and in Thy Name we go".*

THE MARANATHA CALL

THE PROMISED RETURN

To Sardis, the coming of the Lord was given as a warning, a warning to a church which had lost its way. To the church at Philadelphia, the promise of the Lord's coming was like a ray of light in a dark world of gathering gloom.

In the parable of the wise and foolish virgins (Matthew 25), the cry, "The bridegroom cometh" went forth at midnight. Today, we are living in just that hour. Down through the history of the church, little was heard of the coming of Christ. However, that climate has now changed, and the cry has gone forth, 'Maranatha – the Lord is coming!'

This clarion cry has brought hope and new life to the persecuted church, and to believers everywhere as they see the forces of evil making inroads everywhere. At the same time, there is the realisation that, with the return of Christ, this day of grace will have come to its end; no second chance will be given to those who have rejected Christ. This realisation acts as a spur to the missionary church, which is ever thankful for open doors.

The Private Return

As noticed in the letter to Sardis, there is this twofold aspect of the Lord's return. In Philadelphia, the Lord reminds them that He is coming quickly (verse 11). This is the blessed hope of the Church and is the same message which completes the canon of Holy Scripture: "He which testifieth these things saith, Surely I come quickly. Amen. Even so, come, Lord Jesus" (Revelation 22:20). These words should be writ large in every company of believers. They would give each one that sense of urgency and sharpen the edge of all activity for God.

The personal return of the Lord Jesus will be the culmination of all Christian activity. This event will not be delegated to any other, not even to the angels who have been ministering to the church for the past 2,000 years. It will be the Lord Himself who will descend from heaven with a shout, with the voice of the archangel and the trump of God (1 Thessalonians 4:13-18). Unto Him will the gathering of the people be (Genesis 49:10). And so the day of grace will be brought to an end. Philadelphia responded to this challenge – and so must we!

The Public Return

Long years ago, earth's dark night was broken when the angels proclaimed the good news to the shepherds in the fields of Bethlehem. One day, and one day soon, earth's dark night will once again be broken by a heavenly display of glory. It will be vastly different to that seen by the shepherds. The angels will be there, but together with them, the whole host of the redeemed! And in the midst...oh, what a glorious sight! Our precious Lord, no longer the rejected One, no longer the despised Nazarene, but in majestic splendour, crowned with brightest glory, "all wreaths of empire met upon His brow"!

Then our Lord Jesus will return in triumph to take His place upon the throne of David in the holy city of Jerusalem.

> *Lo, He comes from heaven descending,*
> *Once for favoured sinners slain,*
> *Thousand, thousand saints attending*
> *Swell the triumph of His train.*
> *Hallelujah!*
> *Jesus comes, and comes to reign.*

THE MAJESTIC CROWNING

DIVINE APPROBATION

There may be conflict today, but crowning tomorrow awaits the missionary church! Notice how great is the approbation of the Lord Himself: "Because thou hast kept the word of my patience, I also will keep thee from the hour of temptation, which shall come upon all the world, to try them that dwell upon the earth" (verse 10).

DISPLAYED APPELLATION

To the overcomer, there are yet more wonderful promises from the Lord: "Him that overcometh will I make a pillar in the temple of my God…and I shall write upon him the name of my God, and the name of the city of my God…and I will write upon him my new name" (verse 12).

Philadelphia represents the faithful church, displaying brotherly love, showing forth all that has the Lord's commendation. As such, Philadelphia is representative of the true church today, the little flock for whom Christ died. What a privilege to be inscribed with the Lord's own name throughout eternity. This reception of divine appellation is not so much for deeds as for faithfulness, for keeping the word of His patience.

Dramatic Acclamation

In the cave of Adullam, David gathered around himself those who were outcasts, those derided by their neighbours (1 Samuel 22:1,2). They were faithful to him in his rejection. The day came when David was crowned king. In that day, those who had shared his rejection then shared his glory. Our Lord is now rejected, but the crowning day is coming! All those who have owned His name and, in this way, shared His rejection, will then share His glory.

That will be dramatic acclamation indeed! Until that day dawns, an open door is set before us. We must accept the challenge it presents.

9. Laodicea

Laodicea, whose history dates back to the 3rd century BC, now lies in ruins. It was located in a most strategic position, at the crossroads of both north-south and east-west traffic. It was just 10 miles from the city of Colosse. Paul's letter to the Colossians has four references to Laodicea. It soon became a wealthy city; it might be called a get-rich-quick city. It was famous for three things: its banks, its linen and wool industry, and its medical school. There are implicit references to these three activities in the Lord's words to Laodicea (Revelation 3:18).

Just across the valley was Hieropolis with its hot water springs. However, as this water reached Laodicea, it had lost its heat and become lukewarm. It would make anyone who drank it sick (compare 3:16).

Chronologically, this church reflects the church in the 21st century and, as such, has a very pertinent and sobering message for us today. That message may be considered under three headings: the day, the desire, the door.

The Day

The End Times Tempo

As already stated, this is a message for our times. Many Christians believe that Scripture shows us plainly that we are living in the last days before the return of the Lord Jesus.

Perhaps the most telling sign that we are, indeed, in these last days is seen in the return of the Jewish people to their ancient Land, and the restoration of the State of Israel in 1947. Then came the unification of Jerusalem in 1967. We have also witnessed the resurrection of the Hebrew language, the "pure language" of Zephaniah 3:9. Similarly, Jeremiah foretells, "They shall use this speech in the land of Judah and in the cities thereof, when I shall bring again their captivity" (31:23). How exciting this is! Just think – if Moses walked down the Jaffa road in Jerusalem today, he would be able to understand much of what he would read. Some words, such as televisia and telefon, would puzzle him!

The Lord Jesus has left us another extremely telling sign: "And [Jesus] spake to them a parable; Behold the fig tree and all the trees; when they now shoot forth, ye see and know of your own selves that summer is now nigh at hand. So likewise ye, when ye see these things come to pass, know ye that the kingdom of God is nigh at hand" (Luke 21:29-31). In this parable, we have not just the fig tree putting forth its leaves (speaking of Israel), but all the trees (speaking of the nations of the world). Never before in world history have so many nations declared their desire for independence. The peoples of the African continent, the islands of the Pacific, even Scotland and Wales – all these have exhibited strong nationalistic tendencies.

Yes, the end times tempo is gathering momentum. It shows that urgency must be the keynote of the Church's message.

The End Times Temperature

The accusation levelled at the church in Laodicea was that it was lukewarm. Lukewarmness is a process of going from hot to cold – a tepid condition of the church fellowship which once had been on fire for the Lord. But now, "neither cold nor hot" (3:16). What a true characteristic this is of our present age when the cross of Christ is no longer regarded as a vital part of the Gospel! Dr. George Carey, former Archbishop of Canterbury, puts it thus: "Therapy is replacing Christianity and this cannot provide healing to our broken world".

The end result is rejection by God. It is expressed in dramatic terms: "'I will spew you out of My mouth', says the Lord". This warning is not given here to unbelievers, but to members of a professing church!

The End Times Testimony

Some years ago, a famous cartoon depicted a cliff top scene. The peoples of the world were walking in line to the cliff edge, and falling to their death. Nearby, the church was shown sitting down on the grass, making daisy chains! We need to heed the challenge:

> *Where other lords beside Thee hold their unhindered sway,*
> *Where forces that defied Thee, defy Thee still today,*
> *With none to heed their crying for life, and love, and light,*
> *Unnumbered souls are dying and pass into the night.*
> *From cowardice defend us, from lethargy awake!*
> *Forth on Thine errands send us to labour for Thy sake.*

(Frank Houghton)

Significantly, the midnight cry found both the wise and the foolish virgins fast asleep (Matthew 25:5). Let us heed the cry and wake up to proclaim the life giving news to a dying world! The time is short! "Behold, now is the accepted time; behold, now is the day of salvation" (2 Corinthians 6:2).

The Desire

Come – Buy Gold

The prosperity of Laodicea was based on a desire for wealth, for fine clothes, and for eye medicaments. These desires provide the basis for the threefold assault of Satan – "For all that is in the world, the lust of the flesh, and the lust of the eyes, and the pride of life, is not of the Father, but is of the world" (1 John 2:16). These three have resulted in the downfall of man ever since the garden of Eden. Eve succumbed to their attraction: "And when the woman saw that the tree was good for food, and that it was pleasant to the eyes, and a tree to be desired to make one wise, she took..." (Genesis 3:6). When Jesus was tempted in the wilderness, Satan confronted Him with the same threefold attack (Luke 4:1-12).

In Laodicea, we see yet again the same satanic strategy. So it will ever be, and never more so than today. To be forewarned is to be forearmed, and the Lord Jesus has shown us how to deal with the situation – by the Word of God, the Sword of the Spirit. To do this, we need constantly to keep that Word in our hearts, ready for use.

The result of a materialistic society is a blunted desire for the things of God. Present day affluence blinds men to the need for preparation for life after death. We need to take this warning to heart – to come...buy...genuine wealth. It can be purchased without money, without price (Isaiah 55:1). The words of the Lord Jesus still challenge us today:

"Lay up for yourselves treasures in heaven" (Matthew 6:19).

Come – Buy Clothing

The hallmark of these letters to the seven churches is the directness of the message. The Lord comes straight to the point, leaving no ambiguity in the minds of the readers. "Poor, and blind, and naked" is the accusation levelled at the Laodiceans (3:17). This is straight talking indeed to a people who specialised in banking, in medical treatments, and in the clothing trade!

Throughout the word of God, the Holy Spirit leaves us in no doubt as to where we stand in the eyes of heaven. "Our righteousnesses are as filthy rags", thunders the seer of Israel (Isaiah 64:6). Then, in the New Testament, we have the telling parable of the wedding feast. The challenge still presents itself: "Friend, how camest thou in hither not having a wedding garment?" (Matthew 22:12). The wedding garment had been made freely available, but the offer had been refused. We need this heavenly dress if we are to enter into God's presence. We can receive it only as the gift of God. Christ alone is our righteousness, as the hymn reminds us:

> *Jesus, the Lord, our righteousness!*
> *Our beauty Thou, our glorious dress!*
> *Midst flaming worlds in this arrayed,*
> *With joy shall we lift up the head.*

> *This spotless robe the same appears*
> *In new creation's endless years;*
> *No age can change its glorious hue;*
> *The robe of Christ is ever new.*

Till we behold thee on the throne,
In Thee we boast, in Thee alone,
Our beauty this, our glorious dress,
Jesus the Lord, our righteousness.

(Count von Zinzendorf)

As in Laodicea, so today, the Lord knows our state. He still calls, "Buy of me…white raiment, that thou mayest be clothed" (3:18). The call is so relevant to this present age, when so many believe that their self-sufficiency is good enough to warrant a place in heaven.

COME – BUY EYE-SALVE

"Blinded by the god of this world", proclaims Paul (2 Corinthians 4:4). Spiritual blindness prevents a clear picture of what awaits the unbeliever once this life is over. The Laodiceans were able to cope with physical eye problems, but the Lord now tells them that they are spiritually blind. Despite all that Satan can do to a fallen humanity, the Lord Jesus has all the resources to meet the need. But He awaits our response. The invitation has a time factor. It will be withdrawn at the coming of Christ. As believers, we still need to heed this call. We need to be able to view things around us as God sees them.

THE DOOR

PLEADING FOR A RESPONSE

"Behold, I stand at the door, and knock" (3:20). How akin this is to a scene in Song of Solomon 5:2. "Open to me", the Bridegroom calls to His beloved. But the bride is asleep, and when she awakes and opens the door, the Bridegroom has gone. "And then for cause of absence, my troubled soul I scanned", wrote Samuel Rutherford, when he felt the absence of his Lord. The bride hastens to restore communion and, at the same time, declares her love for her Beloved: "My Beloved is white and ruddy, the chiefest among ten thousand...I am my Beloved's, and my Beloved is mine" (5:10; 6:3). She rejoices as communion is restored.

The Lord Jesus seeks the undivided love of His bride. He gave His all to procure her. He knows that, even in a lukewarm church, there are those who truly love Him. Samuel Rutherford captures the feelings of the bride:

> *Oh! I am my Beloved's and my Beloved is mine,*
> *He brings a poor vile sinner into His house of wine.*
> *I stand upon His merit, I know no other stand*
> *Not e'en where glory dwelleth in Immanuel's land.*

The only cure for lukewarmness is a readmitted Christ. We will call this door the door of *devotion*.

PROMISE OF COMMUNION

There are many other doors in Scripture, but a further three are worthy of mention here.

The first is the door of *deliverance*. This one had a blood-sprinkled lintel: "And they shall take of the blood, and strike it on the two side posts and on the upper door post of the houses, wherein they shall eat it...and the blood shall be to you for a token upon the houses where ye are: and when I see the blood, I will pass over you" (Exodus 12:7,13). This was the door of freedom from the slavery of Egypt. We, too, pass out of the darkness of sin's dominion through a doorway sprinkled with blood – the blood of our Passover lamb, Christ (1 Corinthians 5:7).

Forty years later, the Israelites passed through their first door of this new freedom – the door of *dedication*. Having lived in booths during their wilderness wanderings, they are now in the land of promise. No longer would they live in booths, but in houses. As they pass through the doors of these houses, they are reminded of their responsibility. They have been redeemed; now they must live up to their new found liberty: "Hear, O Israel: The LORD our God is one LORD: and thou shalt love the LORD thy God with all thine heart, and with all thy soul, and with all thy might. And these words, which I command thee this day, shall be in thine heart…and thou shalt write them upon the posts of thy house, and on thy gates" (Deuteronomy 6:4-9).

In Jewish households today, these words are still inscribed on a tiny scroll, and placed within a small box, called a mezuzah. This is fixed at an angle, just above shoulder height, on the right hand door post. It will be seen at the entrance of the house and also on the door post of every room, except the bathroom. Thus the mezuzah is a constant reminder of the presence of God and, very especially, a witness to every visitor that here is a household where God is worshipped and obeyed.

In my family household, my father insisted that there should be an indication in every room that it was a household where the Lord Jesus was honoured and worshipped. Passing through this door of *dedication*, our lives should be a living and wholehearted testimony to what the Lord has done for us: "I am crucified with Christ: nevertheless I live; yet not I, but Christ liveth in me: and the life which I now live in the flesh I live by the faith of the Son of God, who loved me, and gave himself for me" (Galatians 2:20).

We come now to the third door, the door of *decision*: "Behold, I stand at the door, and knock: if any man hear my voice, and open the door, I will come in to him, and will sup with him, and he with me" (3:20). Here is a wonderful promise of daily communion and also of that special communion we have with Him at the Lord's supper. It reminds us, too, of the coming marriage supper of the Lamb (Revelation 19:9).

Laodicea reflects our modern age, with its utter indifference to the things of God, with its utter lukewarmness, even in church life. The Lord is gracious. He calls today to individuals within such a church to open themselves up to His love and to His abiding presence. To those who respond to Him, there can be no higher promise, no higher honour can be imagined: "To him that overcometh will I grant to sit with me in my throne, even as I also overcame, and am set down with my Father in his throne" (3:21). "This saying promises the last and final privilege; it concludes equally effectively the crown of seven promises to the conquerors and the seven letters themselves" (Lohmeyer).

We look in the mirror – what do we see? We listen – what do we hear? Our response must be to repent, to open the door and to commit ourselves fully to His abiding presence.

O patient, spotless One
Our hearts in meekness train,
To bear Thy yoke, and learn of Thee
That we may rest obtain.

Jesus, Thou art enough
The mind and heart to fill;
Thy patient life — to calm the soul;
Thy love — its fear dispel.

O fix our earnest gaze
So wholly, Lord, on Thee
That with Thy beauty occupied
We may transformed be.

(C.A. Bernstein)

10. A Collective View of the Seven Churches

The individual messages to each of the seven churches have been looked at in some detail. It will be interesting and instructive to look now at some general features of the seven churches together. The following particular aspects will be considered:

1. The presentation of the Lord to each church.
2. The warnings of the Lord to each church.
3. The promises of the Lord to the overcomer in each church.

The Presentation of the Lord

In each of the seven letters, the Lord introduces Himself in a different manner. Each style of introduction is pertinent to the message addressed to the individual church. In chapter 1, John was given an initial vision of Christ in majesty. Now, in these messages, we have another sevenfold picture of our risen Lord Jesus. In this portrayal, we see Him as He surveys the Church militant.

This aspect of our Lord's activity is worthy of our attention. It follows His ascension and is prior to His return to this earth. During this period, He is interceding for us as our Great High Priest (Hebrews 4:14-16). He is also preparing a place for us (John 14:2). He will then return and usher in His Messianic reign. However, in Revelation 2 and 3, we are given a clear sevenfold composite picture of our Lord's present activity as Head of His Church.

Ephesus

To the church at Ephesus, the Lord appears as the *Director*. "These things saith He that holdeth the seven stars in His right hand, who walketh in the midst of the seven golden lampstands" (2:1). Here is a timely reminder to the church at Ephesus that it, together with the other six churches, derives its life from fellowship in the Lord Jesus. They are subject to Him; they are upheld by Him; they receive their power from Him. But they also come under His searching scrutiny!

So today, in our assembly life, we need to remember that we stand in the same light. We are under His direction. The Lord is still walking in the midst of the lampstands.

The basic problem at Ephesus was that they were allowing a gulf to open up between themselves and their Lord. In this way, they were no longer responding to His direction. A happily married couple are sensitive to each other because of the love which binds them together. The church at Ephesus was losing that bridal love, so that sensitivity had lost its edge.

Christina Rosetti put her finger on the problem when she wrote:

> *Lord, Thou art life, though I be dead;*
> *Love's fire Thou art, however cold I be.*

> *Nor heaven have I, nor place to lay my head,*
> *Nor home, but Thee.*

There must be that living, close relationship between the church and her Head. He directs. We must respond, or love's fire will be extinguished.

SMYRNA

To the church at Smyrna, He appears as the *Defeater*. "These things saith the first and the last, which was dead, and is alive" (2:8). What an encouragement and comfort these words must have been to this suffering and persecuted church! Here is a glorious reminder of the triumph of that first Easter Day. The Lord had defeated death and Satan. The tomb was empty; the Lord had risen to die no more! He is the Victor; He had conquered!

As a consequence of His victory, all who place their trust in Him share that victory. "Death is swallowed up in victory. O death, where is thy sting? O grave, where is thy victory?" (1 Corinthians 15:54,55). As the suffering of the believers at Smyrna intensified, they were reminded that the Lord Himself had been into death and triumphed. He is the Alpha and the Omega. He knew all that they were having to endure.

"Weeping may endure for a night, but joy cometh in the morning" (Psalm 30:5). This blessed assurance still holds good today for Christians under persecution, or in trouble, throughout the world. The abiding presence of the Saviour is there to give strength to all who are passing through such times. There is always a great danger that, in these circumstances, it is so easy for the enemy to undermine our faith, just as he tried with Job.

> *When hosts of sin encompass me,*
> *When tempted not to trust in Thee,*

*Open my eyes that I may see
Jesus is nearer and stronger.*

May this be our constant prayer during times of stress. Such an arrow prayer will bring spiritual strength and a blessed assurance that we are on the victory side. Christian, claim the victory which our Lord has won! Claim His precious blood which assures us that we shall overcome! Above all, let there ever be a praising in our hearts. The power of prayer will result in praise. C.H.Spurgeon aptly put it this way:

*Prayers and praises go in pairs;
They have praises who have prayers.*

PERGAMUM

To the church at Pergamum, He appears as the *Discerner*. "These things saith He that hath the sharp sword with two edges" (2:12). We are all familiar with the figure of justice with sword in hand. Here the Lord presents Himself as the administrator of justice. He is indeed a discerner of what is happening within His Church. Let us never forget this!

In this capacity, He comes to deal with the false teachers, those "birds of the air" who have nestled in the branches of the unnatural growth within this church at Pergamum. The Lord is a jealous God. He will not tolerate false churchism. This comes as a sharp reminder to those Christian fellowships who pay little heed to the real position of those who seek fellowship within the church community.

Fellowship within the assembly is not a free for all. There are strict parameters which must be adhered to. At the close of his Gospel, John declares that he has written "that ye might believe that Jesus is the Christ, the Son of God;

and that believing ye might have life through his name" (20:31). This is the touchstone. Confession of faith in our Lord Jesus is essential, and such evidence must be forthcoming before the hand of fellowship is given. Such evidence was not sought for at Pergamum – hence the two edged sword.

There must never be a watering down of the Gospel message. "Repentance toward God, and faith toward our Lord Jesus Christ" (Acts 20:21) lies at its heart. When a soul confesses Christ in all sincerity, then he is received into the fellowship of believers. There can be no other ground for reception into fellowship. The church at Pergamum had no such yardstick. The Lord had to act against their looseness. The use of His two edged sword clearly shows the discernment which was needed. In these closing days of the Church's history, we also must stand firm and be ever vigilant for those "grievous wolves" who seek to destroy the flock (Acts 20:29).

THYATIRA

To the church at Thyatira, He appears as the *Destroyer*. "These things saith the Son of God, who hath His eyes like unto a flame of fire, and His feet are like fine brass" (2:18). To this church, and to this church alone, the Lord presents Himself as the Son of God. This is an assertion of His power and authority. He has to deal with an evil for which there are no remedial measures. Nothing but judgment remains. It is to emphasise this that He uses His title of supreme authority. His burning eyes penetrate into the hidden depths of the heart, and into the very depths of a fellowship where there is gross corruption. He declares that death will come to those who have fallen for the teachings of Jezebel.

A COLLECTIVE VIEW OF THE SEVEN CHURCHES

As Head of His Church, the Lord still demands purity today. He will act to ensure this. He is the Lord. Throughout these letters, we have a recurring theme. The Lord is looking for singleness of heart, for a company of believers whose eyes are fixed on Him, and who will not tolerate any compromise with the world or with wrong doctrine. In short, the Lord is looking for those who have within them the spirit of Elijah (1 Kings 18:21).

SARDIS

To the church at Sardis, He appears as the *Detector*. "He that hath the seven spirits of God, and the seven stars" (3:1). This message is a most solemn reminder to a dead church. It sounds a trumpet blast. The double use of 'seven' emphasises the display of His power in all its fullness.

Despite any smoke screen which the church may use as a cover up, the Lord has probed the situation to its very depths. Dead though the church may be, the Lord has the perfect answer for those within the church whose desire it is to hold fast and repent.

PHILADELPHIA

To the church at Philadelphia, He appears as the *Defender*. "He that is holy, He that is true, He that hath the key of David, He that openeth, and no man shutteth; and shutteth, and no man openeth" (3:7). What strength these opening words must have given to the church at Philadelphia! Here was a church eager and ready to spread the new Christian faith, eager to reach out beyond its borders. At the same time, the members were conscious of their own weakness, particularly as they looked on the pagan world all around them.

Now comes this precious word from their Lord, reminding them that He is the holy and the true. These are the attributes of God Himself. The words used are similar to those used to describe Eliakim, a prophetic anticipation of Christ Himself (Isaiah 22:22). To the church in the 21st century, this age-old message is ever new and relevant. So Paul can exclaim triumphantly, "If *God* be for us, who can be against us?" (Romans 8:31).

This is a timeless message to encourage all those who are seeking to take the Gospel message to a lost world, to all those who are seeking to obey the great commission, "Go" (Matthew 28:19). "How shall they hear without a preacher? And how shall they preach, except they be sent?" (Romans 10:14,15). "Lift up your eyes, and look on the fields; for they are white already to harvest" (John 4:35). "The harvest truly is great, but the labourers are few; pray ye therefore the Lord of the harvest, that He would send forth labourers into His harvest" (Luke 10:2). May we recognise the door which the Lord has opened for us, and go forward in His strength!

Laodicea

To the church at Laodicea, He appears as the *Declarer*. He is "the Amen, the faithful and true witness, the beginning of the creation of God" (3:14). In these words, the Lord declares His essential glory. There are three great statements of fact. In the first, He is the Amen. This is a title of God given in Isaiah 65:16. (Note that the Hebrew word 'Amen' is there translated 'truth'. So the Lord, in the upper room, could declare Himself to be the truth (John 14:6)).

Secondly, as the faithful and true witness, He comes to contrast Himself with the failure of the Laodiceans. With William Kelly, we can declare:

A COLLECTIVE VIEW OF THE SEVEN CHURCHES

*God and Father, we adore Thee
For the Christ, Thine image bright,
In whom all Thy holy nature
Dawned on our once hopeless night.*

*Thou didst send Him as a witness
Of a life beyond compare;
By Thy Spirit we received Him;
Now in Christ how blest we are.*

*For in Christ was life eternal
Once beheld and heard below;
And in Him dwelt all the fullness,
Though in grace He stooped so low.*

Thirdly, He was the beginning of the creation of God. These words take us to Colossians 1:15-20. Here we are reminded that He is the image of the invisible God, the firstborn of every creature. In that position of supremacy, He has been given "a name which is above every name: that at the name of Jesus every knee should bow…and that every tongue should confess that Jesus Christ is Lord, to the glory of God the Father" (Philippians 2:9-11).

As we consider the Lord in these sevenfold glories, let us with deep reverence recognise the activity of the Lord Jesus today as He walks in the midst of the seven golden lampstands, that is, amongst the assemblies of His people. May this deeper understanding of His present activity move us to greater worship and service for Him today!

THE WARNINGS GIVEN TO EACH CHURCH

Solemn warnings were given to five of the seven churches. The churches at Smyrna and Philadelphia received no warnings, but only promises.

To Ephesus, the warning was of *removal*: "I will remove thy lampstand out of his place, except thou repent" (2:5).

To Pergamum, the warning was of *wrath*: "Repent, or else I will come unto thee quickly, and will fight against them with the sword of My mouth" (2:16).

To Thyatira, the warning was of *recompense*: "I will give unto every one of you according to your works" (2:23).

To Sardis, the warning was of *return*: "If therefore thou shalt not watch, I will come on thee as a thief, and thou shalt not know what hour I will come upon thee" (3:3).

To Laodicea, the warning was of *rejection*: "So then because thou art lukewarm, and neither cold nor hot, I will spew thee out of My mouth" (3:16).

These are serious and solemn warnings. They were not given to the world of unbelievers, but rather to those who had been observing all that they believed was expected of them as church members. The disappearance of these churches from history is yet another example of what we learn from the fate of Capernaum, Bethsaida, and Chorazin. These privileged towns had all been visited by Christ. They had all received blessings from Him. Yet they perished in their unbelief.

Our Lord reminded His disciples that "unto whomsoever much is given, of him shall much be required" (Luke 12:48). These assemblies had assumed a place of spiritual privilege. They would have claimed to be a royal priesthood, ambassadors for Christ in a pagan world. No doubt, they all led busy church lives. Much was expected from them but, with the passage of time, serious flaws were coming to light.

In ancient times, when quarrymen, engaged in extracting blocks of marble, discovered that a block had flaws in it, they would sometimes try to conceal the defect by covering the crack with wax, and then selling it as perfect.

Buyers who were aware of this fraudulent practice would ask for an assurance that the block was 'without wax', in Latin 'sine cere' and hence our word 'sincere'.

Some years ago... in Israel, watching flowers being packed for export, it was interesting to see samples being passed under special lighting. The normal effect from this treatment was a bright glow being emitted from the stem of the flower. However, from time to time no glow was apparent. Under Israeli export legislation, flowers for export had to have their stems immersed in a chemical solution. This was to ensure that they would retain their freshness, in view of the time that would elapse before they arrived at the retail florist. To the naked eye, treated and untreated stems looked exactly alike. The lamp revealed the truth! The Lord, surveying the churches with eyes as a flame of fire, reveals all. He can see through the sham, through the make believe. He knows what is sincere and what is not.

Let us be sincere before the Lord so that, like the suffering church at Smyrna and the steadfast church at Philadelphia, there may be nothing in us to call forth the Lord's rebuke. As we ponder over the warnings given to these other 1st century churches, let us make the words of J. Edwin Orr our prayer:

> *Search me, O God, and know my heart today;*
> *Try me, O Lord, and know my thoughts I pray;*
> *See if there be some wicked way in me,*
> *Cleanse me from every sin and set me free.*
>
> *I praise Thee, Lord, for cleansing me from sin;*
> *Fulfil Thy word, and make me pure within;*

Fill me with fire, where once I burned with shame,
Grant my desire to magnify Thy name.

Ephesus and Laodicea both faced the threat of immediate rejection by the Lord, should the warning go unheeded. In these churches, first love for Jesus had evaporated. Ephesus had left their first love; Laodicea had become lukewarm. Nevertheless, an opportunity was given to both to repent and to return to their once privileged position. This must speak to our own hearts today! We know only too well that, where there is a deep love for Jesus, lukewarmness is out of the question.

Differences between believers will inevitably occur in assembly life. Personality clashes are always ready to surface. Then there is the inherent weakness of the flesh, the pride, the lust. It is only when love for Jesus takes preeminence that these fleshly, dominant forces will be forced into submission. Love conquers all!

The warnings to the other three churches are linked to the second coming of the Lord. These warnings are so relevant to today's church, for all the signs around us indicate His near return. Those assemblies who recognise themselves in the Patmos mirror need urgently to consider their position before the Lord. Repeatedly in these messages we have been confronted with the second coming of the Lord. In the light of this, the call to repentance must seriously and urgently be faced head on. Soon the day of grace will come to an end. We must not be ashamed before Him at His coming!

THE PROMISES OF THE LORD TO THE OVERCOMER IN EACH CHURCH

It will be of interest to note the promise given to the overcomer in each church.

A COLLECTIVE VIEW OF THE SEVEN CHURCHES

To Ephesus: "To him that overcometh will I give to eat of the tree of life, which is in the midst of the paradise of God" (2:7).

The keynote of this promise is *survival.*

To Smyrna: "He that overcometh shall not be hurt of the second death" (2:11).

The keynote of this promise is *safety.*

To Pergamum: "To him that overcometh will I give to eat of the hidden manna, and I will give him a white stone, and in the stone a new name written, which no man knoweth saving he that receiveth it" (2:17).

The keynote of this promise is *sufficiency.*

To Thyatira: "And he that overcometh, and keepeth my works unto the end, to him will I give power over the nations; and he shall rule them with a rod of iron; as the vessels of a potter shall they be broken to shivers; even as I received of my Father. And I will give him the morning star" (2:26-28).

The keynote of this promise is *supremacy.*

To Sardis: "He that overcometh, the same shall be clothed in white raiment; and I will not blot out his name out of the book of life, but I will confess his name before my Father, and before his angels" (3:5).

The keynote of this promise is *sanctification.*

To Philadelphia: " Him that overcometh will I make a pillar in the temple of my God, and he shall go no more out; and I will write upon him the name of my God, and the name of the city of my God, which is new Jerusalem, which cometh down out of heaven from my God; and I will write upon him my new name" (3:12).

The keynote of this promise is *standing*.

To Laodicea: "To him that overcometh will I grant to sit with me in my throne, even as I also overcame, and am sat down with my Father in his throne" (3:21).

The keynote of this promise is *sovereign grace*.

A detailed exposition of these promises is not intended. This can readily be found in larger treatises on the book of Revelation. Some comments, however, in line with the general tenor of this book on Patmos, will follow.

At the outset, let us always remember that "all the promises of God in Him are yea, and in Him Amen, unto the glory of God by us" (2 Corinthians 1:20). The Lord is ever gracious. As He walks amidst the lampstands, He is fully aware of the spiritual warfare confronting those who have put their trust in Him. This, of course, was particularly true in the early days of the Church. These seven churches were surrounded by pagan nations who had for centuries worshipped idols and mythological gods. These nations were steeped in superstition. Now a new situation was developing, a new faith was being introduced. In this conflict, these new Christians discovered that the word of God abounded in glorious promises. These promises brought comfort and strength, as well as hope.

In retrospect, however, we realise something of the power of the enemy in that it took only 35 years for the believers in Ephesus to fall from the spiritual heights of blessing, as outlined in their letter from Paul, to the sad situation which we have considered earlier.

In the darkness of the night, Abraham was told by God to lift up his eyes toward heaven (Genesis 15:5). There he saw that the night sky was filled with the light of countless number of stars, each star representing a promise from God. So we also, during the night of this world as we await the break of day, can lift up our heads towards heaven and know that the night sky of the world is alive with the promises of God!

So we can sing:

> *God's promises come true.*
> *Whate'er He says He will do.*
> *My heart no doubt can hold*
> *Of things He has told.*
>
> *I know Your word is sure;*
> *It is a rock secure.*
> *What You say comes about,*
> *This I can never doubt.*
>
> *God's promises are true,*
> *Fulfilment will ensue.*
> *My trust must e'er prevail;*
> *His word can never fail.*
>
> *Whate'er He says He will do;*
> *His word is clear and true.*
> *The waiting may be long,*
> *'Twill end in triumph song.*

(M.Basilea Schlink)

Five basic promises of God to the Children of Israel are encapsulated in Exodus 6:6-8. In a spiritual sense, we are able, through grace, to claim these same promises for ourselves. They are:

1. I will bring you out from under the burden of the Egyptians.
2. I will rid you of their bondage.
3. I will redeem you.

4. I will take you to Me for a people.
5. I will bring you into the land.

Such promises as these must surely cause us to break out into songs of praise and worship. We can rejoice now in the salvation expressed in the first four; we await with joyful expectation the fulfilment of the fifth. Scripture abounds with promises for our earthly pilgrimage today. Our daily walk is garlanded with such promises. Well might we, then, sing:

> *Standing on the promises of Christ my King,*
> *Through eternal ages let His praises ring;*
> *Glory in the highest, I will shout and sing,*
> *Standing on the promises of God.*

However, in the letters to these seven churches, very specific promises are made to those who will be overcomers in the spiritual warfare. In each case, the promise given is particularly relevant to the conditions prevailing in that church. Despite the failures portrayed in five of the seven churches, a word of encouragement is given to those within them who desire to overcome the worldly pressures around them. The mighty conflict being waged in the heavenlies against believers then, and today, can not be underestimated. The battle is fierce. Spiritual forces of darkness and evil are engaged in making every attempt to destroy Christian witness and to turn hearts away from God. Overcoming such forces will never be achieved through mere human strength or will-power. To be an overcomer needs divine strength. The whole armour of God, in fact, is essential for protection in this warfare (see Ephesians 6:11-18).

The girdle of truth, the breastplate of righteousness and the sword of the Spirit are all vital components of this armour. The shield, as mentioned by Paul, was not the small circular one which was sometimes used, but rather a long one which covered much of the body. In ancient wars, Spartan mothers told their sons as they left for battle, "Come back carrying your shield, or upon it (i.e. as a stretcher or a bier)". It was a dishonour and a disgrace to be parted from one's shield, whether in life or death.

We must keep like faith and use our shield "to quench all the fiery darts of the wicked" (verse 16).

> *Be valiant, be strong,*
> *Resist the power of sin!*
> *The fight is long, the foe is strong, but you shall win;*
> *For through the power of Christ — the Stronger than the strong —*
> *You shall be more than conqueror.*
> *Be valiant, be strong.*

The promises to the overcomers contained in these letters are not primarily connected to the daily walk of the Christian, but rather look on to the end result. They look forward, in the main, to the eternal day. In this way, they act as an encouragement to believers to press on. Paul could write, "I have fought a good fight, I have finished my course, I have kept the faith: henceforth there is laid up for me a crown of righteousness, which the Lord, the righteous judge, shall give me at that day" (2 Timothy 4:7,8).

We can take courage in the fact that Satan is a defeated foe; yet we recognise, at the same time, that he is described as a roaring lion. So we must ever be sober and vigilant (1 Peter 5:8). Satan's fiery darts seek to penetrate and to take advantage of our human weaknesses. He is only too well aware of our fallibilities!

The promises of Revelation 2,3 reveal so very clearly the love and grace of our Saviour. He loved the Church and gave Himself for it, and now, at its very inception, He sees so much failure creeping in. At times, there is the very denial of everything that He looks for. His longsuffering love goes out to those whose desire it is to respond to this love. It is to these, the overcomers, that the Lord offers such wonderful promises. He reveals the reward which will be theirs if, like Paul, they fight the good fight of faith.

To those at Ephesus, the promise is given of that which was denied to Adam in the Garden of Eden, that earthly paradise. Now in God's paradise, they will be able to eat of the fruit of the tree of life.

The overcomers in the church at Smyrna, having experienced death and suffering, will be given the crown of life.

Hidden manna, a white stone, a new name – all these are promised to the overcomer in Pergamum. It is not at all clear what is exactly meant by the hidden manna. It could refer to what was placed in the Holy Ark (Exodus 16:33; Hebrews 9:4). It might even be an oblique reference to that part of the passover loaf, the afikomen, which was hidden during the passover meal. It was this hidden loaf which the Lord took, announcing that it symbolised His body which was to be given in sacrifice. The white stone, too, has interesting possibilities. At the conclusion of a trial, the jury would hand to the judge either a white or a black stone, depending on the verdict. A white stone was also used to give right of entry to public festivals, or royal assemblies. It also symbolised victory in warfare. Another, and rather beautiful, use of the white stone was a practice known as Tessara Hospitalis. Two friends, soon about to part, would split a white stone in half, each half bearing the name of the other. The halves would then be exchanged, and often passed down the generations. On a future occasion, should the halves be presented, each still bearing the name of the original friend, then a firm friendship would at once be acknowledged.

Highest of all the promises, surely, was that to the overcomers in the apostate church of Laodicea. No higher honour can be imagined. "To share my throne", said the Lord. Sovereign grace indeed!

As stated earlier, these churches provide us with a mirror reflecting the spiritual condition of church life in today's world. The different pictures in each highlight specific recognisable scenarios in the church today. We need to give these serious thought. Should alarm bells ring, then we have, through God's grace, still time, albeit a very short time, to change course.

The Watchword is "Repent!" The night is far spent; the day is at hand (Romans 13:12).

A Summary of the Seven Churches

Ephesus .... coldness

Smyrna .... crossbearing

Pergamum .... collaborating

Thyatira .... compromising

Sardis .... corpselike

Philadelphia .... committed

Laodicea .... Christless

These seven churches have now passed into history. Their modern counterparts, however, live on and are with us today. Let us look carefully into the mirror presented to us from this little island of Patmos, and ask ourselves, "What does the reflection tell *us*?"

As John's vision on this island came to an end, he wrote, "He which testifieth these things saith, Surely I come quickly. Amen, Even so, come, Lord Jesus. The grace of our Lord Jesus Christ be with you all. Amen" (22:20,21). May His grace, His love, His Shalom, shine through us as we go forward on our pilgrim journey!

PATMOS SPEAKS TODAY

PATMOS SPEAKS TODAY

BY THE SAME AUTHOR

THE HOLY LAND: A PERSONAL PILGRIMAGE
ISBN-13: 978-0-901860-15-6
ISBN-10: 0-901860-15-8;
Scripture Truth Publications
75 pages; Paperback; June 1997

Printed in the United Kingdom
by Lightning Source UK Ltd.
118694UK00001B/13-30